The Basic Guide to

SURVIVAL

The Basics of Faith — SIX ESSENTIALS — FOR THE BELIEVER

Rob Cresswell

This edition 'The Believer's Guide to Survival'
printed 2022

Previously published as 'What next Jesus?'

© Copyright 2017 – Rob Cresswell

All rights reserved. No part of this publication may be reproduced, stored in a retrieval system, or transmitted in any form or by any means, electronic, mechanical, photocopying or otherwise, without the prior written consent of the author.

All Scripture quotations are taken from the New International Version © 1973, 1978, 1984 by International Bible Society.

Unless marked NKJV in which case:
Scripture taken from the New King James Version.
Copyright © 1982 by Thomas Nelson, Inc.
Used by permission. All rights reserved.

ISBN 13: 9780957264229
ISBN 10: 0957264224

Visit: www.SpiritLifestyle.com
for more resources.

Contents

                                          page

Introduction	5
1: air Christ in you, the hope of glory	7
2: water Out of his heart will flow streams of living water	19
3: food Jesus said, "I am the bread of life"	31
4: shelter You are a temple of the Holy Spirit	43
5: purpose God… put him in the Garden of Eden to work it and take care of it	57
6: community Let us not give up meeting together	69
afterword	83
further reading	85
about the author	88

Note on Bible references:

There are footnotes throughout this booklet that look like this:

a Rom 10:13

These footnotes are abbreviated Bible references which verify that the statement in the text is Biblical. The above example would be found in the book of Romans chapter 10 and verse 13.

introduction

First things first. I am so delighted that you have recognised Jesus as your personal Saviour, confessed to Him that you are a sinner and put your trust in Him to save you from hell and for heaven. You may have done this very suddenly or it may have become your conviction over a period of time. In any case, welcome to the family, for "Everyone who calls on the name of the Lord will be saved[a]." The reason I say this is because this booklet is not about how to become a Christian. I'm going to assume you have already made that decision and confessed and acted upon it. If you haven't made that decision yet, can I urge you to do so, it is the most important decision you will ever make.

So let's get down to business. Welcome to your new life in Jesus. This booklet is written to give you an overview of some of the basics you are going to need to enable you to thrive and grow in your faith. I have met many people like you. You may feel like everything has changed. Perhaps you are enjoying the wonderful relief of forgiveness. Whether you feel different or not

a Joel 2:28, Acts 2:21, Rom 10:13

doesn't really matter. What matters is that through faith you have been made new. 1 Peter 1:23-24 says **"For you have been born again, not of perishable seed, but of imperishable, through the living and enduring word of God"**. I imagine a clarity in your eyes that tells me you have a new heart that is alive to God. At the same time your head is probably flooding with questions: "I don't understand this? What about that?" There is so much you do not know and you are HUNGRY...

Whatever your background, whether you are completely new to Christianity and church or you have been familiar with it for years, there are certain fundamentals of the Christian faith you will find helpful to understand. It is true that there is a vast spectrum of expressions and traditions within Christianity but the essentials remain the same.

In this booklet I have used the metaphor of physical needs for life as an illustration of spiritual needs for life. Like most metaphors it is not meant as an absolute standard. My hope is that it will simply provide a framework upon which to build spiritual principles to help you live out your faith in Jesus.

Chapter 1

air

Christ in you, the hope of glory

One of the most elemental requirements for the human body to live is oxygen. Without oxygen, brain cells will very quickly start to deteriorate and die... we don't last long without an air supply.

The first thing a new born baby needs to do is open its mouth, inhale and begin to breathe with its lungs. Now that you have put your trust in Jesus for your salvation it's as if you've taken your first big breath of 'spiritual oxygen' and drawn eternal life into your soul. The truth is that you now have the abiding presence of God in your life[a]. You may or may not feel different but this truth affects everything about you, particularly your identity before God. You were lost but now you are found[b], you were dead but now you are alive[a], you

a John 14:23, b Luke 15:24,

were spiritually blind but now you can see[b]. You have been adopted into God's family[c], you are a part of the royal household of the King of Kings[d]. The Apostle Paul described it like this: "Christ in you the hope of glory." Colossians 1:27

Just like physical breathing, you are now sustained spiritually by the life giving presence of Jesus by virtue of the Holy Spirit living in you. Your eternal life has begun[e].

Did you feel different after you asked Jesus into your life? Most people feel that something has changed. However, just as we're not always conscious of our physical breathing and it becomes a normal part of living, sometimes you will be aware of His presence within you and sometimes you won't. That doesn't mean Jesus has left you. It is just like breathing, we often forget that the air around us is sustaining our life, that doesn't mean the air is no longer there. In the same way, Jesus is now living in you by His Holy Spirit. He is there because you invited Him in.

In the beginning: God breathed life

Genesis is the first book of the Bible and is all about new beginnings. Genesis chapter 2 verse 7 says, "The Lord God formed the man from the dust of the ground

a Romans 8:10, b John 9:39, c John 1:12,13, d 1 Peter 2:9, e John 17:3

and breathed into his nostrils the breath of life, and the man became a living being."

This verse from Genesis gives us a wonderful picture of intimacy, as at the point of creating mankind, God breathed His own life-giving spirit into the man that He had formed from the earth. After forming Adam's body, God got face to face with him and imparted His own life-giving breath into his nostrils[a]. We can imagine that the first thing Adam saw as he opened his eyes was the face of his Creator smiling back at him. In the same way, in the early days of your new life in Christ you need to bond with your heavenly Father by enjoying His delight in you.

I remember when my children were very small babies they would sleep on my chest and we were so close up to each other that we would breathe each other's air. These were precious times that bonded our new relationship as father and child. Genesis also tells us that Adam was made in God's image or likeness; you were created for intimacy and friendship with God.

Not religion but relationship

For the Christian, spiritual life is sustained by the indwelling presence of the Holy Spirit. At its heart, Christianity is not a religion or even an historical event.

a Genesis 2:7

It's a relationship, a trusting relationship between you and your Creator God. When you confessed Jesus to be your Saviour He came to dwell in your body by His Holy Spirit and made you alive to God[a]. In the New Testament Paul refers to this spiritual birth as a 'new creation'[b] and reading the Genesis account it's easy to see why. When the Holy Spirit comes to live in you it's like God breathing new life into Adam. You have become a new creation and you can behold your God in a wonderful new way.

Because Jesus promises that He will never leave you or forsake you[c], you can utterly depend on the indwelling Holy Spirit to be like a source of life-giving oxygen supply. Breathe deeply of Him any time and any place, He is your life now.

> ***Something to do:*** *Allow yourself to become aware of your physical breathing right now. As you breathe in begin to thank the Lord for His presence within you by His Holy Spirit. Let your breathing go a little deeper and slower... As you breathe in tell the Lord how much you appreciate and love Him. As you breathe out, let some of the cares and worries of the day go to Jesus. Have intentional thoughts about those cares and concerns going to Him. Then repeat the process of breathing in and receiving his peace and presence. Do that for a while and then give Him thanks for your new life in Christ.*

a John 14:23, b 2 Cor 5:17, c Matt 28:20

Reunited

Just as your body is designed to need air, you were created to need the presence of God in your life. This is how it was for Adam and Eve in the Garden of Eden. The Bible says that God walked in the garden in the cool of the day with them[a]. They enjoyed open unbroken fellowship with their Creator God.

The Genesis story goes on to tell us that tragically this beautiful relationship was broken by deception and mistrust. If you read Genesis chapter 3 you will see that the serpent suggested to Eve that God was a withholding God who was keeping something good from them. In this way he persuaded them not to trust God and as a result both Adam and Eve ate the forbidden fruit. It was their doubt and mistrust of God's goodness that led to the disobedience that followed.

The result of this disobedience was catastrophic for the human race. It is an undeniable fact that we live in a messed up world. If you don't believe me, take a look at the news headlines today. The Bible says that people are wicked in every way and that not one is righteous; we have all fallen short of the glory of God[b]. From the worst of us to the best of us, human nature is corrupt and in need of redemption. We need God's help to get us out of this mess. We need a saviour.

a Gen 3:8, b Rom 3:23

This is where Jesus comes in, because He is not merely a created being but the Son of God Himself. You may remember the Christmas song 'O Come all ye faithful' which has the line, "Begotten not created". This means that Jesus was unique because He was born the perfect, sinless man. He was and is both man and God. John the Baptist declared, "Behold, the lamb of God who takes away the sin of the world."[a] Jesus came to make all things new[b].

About the Trinity of God

Scripture is clear that God is three persons with one divine nature: God - Father, Son and Holy Spirit. Each one relates to the others with complete unity and love. A useful picture is to think of how water can be ice, liquid or steam; the same substance with three very distinct characteristics.

Trust

The Biblical word for Jesus' death in our place is the 'atonement'. It's not possible to fully explain the atonement in this little booklet but I recommend you get a good book on it (see 'recommended further reading' at the back of this booklet). It's enough to say here that the effect of the atonement is like stepping up onto your own execution platform only to find that

a John 1:29, b Rev 21:5

someone is standing in your place. That someone of course is Jesus.

Jesus put off the privileges of His divinity and came down to earth for many reasons[a]. One of them was to reveal to people the nature of God and to demonstrate to us what it was like for a man to live a life of complete trust and obedience to God. Jesus said, "The world must learn that I love the Father and that I do exactly what my Father has commanded me."[b] Because of this the Apostle Paul, one of the most prolific New Testament writers, describes Jesus as the second Adam[c].

As a new Christian you will quickly find that this issue of your trust in God has the biggest impact on the depth and effectiveness of your life in Christ.

Proverbs 3:5-6 says: "Trust in the Lord with all your heart, and lean not on your own understanding; in all your ways acknowledge Him, and He shall direct your paths." NKJV

The book of Proverbs in the Bible is a collection of wise sayings and the best advice I can give you as you start your 'new life in Christ' adventure is the wisdom of this little verse. Set your heart on serving God. Make knowing Him your daily goal. Settle it in your heart that you will be humble and teachable before Him. You may

a See Philippians 2:6-11, b John 14:31, c Rom 5:18,19

not get all the answers you want as fast as you would like but remember to, "Trust in the Lord with all your heart" and true understanding will surely come to you.

Knowing the God who is love

Moses, a well known character in the Bible who knew God in a special 'face to face' way, knew that it was the Lord's desire to speak directly into all men's hearts and he looked forward to the day when this would happen[a]. As a new Christian it's good and proper for you to read and learn from those who are ahead of you in their spiritual growth and it's also wonderful to see God meet your needs through answered prayer. However never let someone else or even what God can do for you take the place of your own personal heart knowledge of God. That is by far the greater prize. We all come to God with needs. I wonder what yours are? Meeting these needs is important to God but if they are the basis for your relationship with Him there is a danger that once you have got what you want, you will forget about Him. Or what if you don't get immediate answers? How long will you serve Him then? We cannot come to God with terms and conditions. All we can bring to God's table is a desire to know His love - that is all He requires of you[a]. I hope you will learn to love God for who He is and not just what He can do for

a Num 11:29

you. I guarantee the more you get to know Him, the easier this will become.

How can I be sure I'm saved?

The basis of your 'trust in the Lord' is the finished work of Jesus on the cross. He died for you. You are accepted and forgiven, this is the foundation of your faith. This means you can be sure of your salvation because it isn't about your ability but about His faithfulness. In Colossians chapter one Paul says that we can now rejoice and praise our Father God because *He has qualified us* to live in the Kingdom of light; the Kingdom of His Son Jesus Christ[b]. Your new life of righteousness (being right with God) has nothing to do with what you have done to attain or deserve, but is simply a free gift of God (often called grace). That is the good news of the gospel of Jesus Christ. You have received that gift through trust (or faith) in God. Even now, just let some thankfulness bubble up from inside and find expression on your lips. Thank the Lord for what He has done for you on the cross. Let praise and worship, thankfulness and joy begin to flow to God from your heart.

a Isaiah 55:1-3, b Col 1:12

Something to do

The Psalmist says:

"Praise the Lord, O my soul; all my inmost being, praise his holy name. Praise the Lord, O my soul, and forget not all his benefits - who forgives all your sins and heals all your diseases, who redeems your life from the pit and crowns you with love and compassion, who satisfies your desires with good things so that your youth is renewed like the eagle's."

Psalm 103:1-5

Why not read this song of thankfulness as if it were your song of thankfulness to God? Honour and respect for God and a praising heart are the beginning of wisdom[a]. You will find that joining in acts of worship with other believers is a wonderful blessing but it is important to learn how to worship God in Spirit and truth for yourself first. Begin to make it your practice to let praise and thanks come easily to your lips throughout the day; honour God for His goodness as you wake in the morning and for His faithfulness as you fall asleep at night.

---

a Ps 111:10

Questions to think about:

1. When did you give your life to Jesus? Was it a gradual experience or sudden and unexpected? What has changed since you called on the name of Jesus?

2. Why is Christianity primarily a relationship?

3. Proverbs 3 verses 5-6 say, "In all your ways acknowledge Him". What do you think this means to you in practice?

Chapter 2

water

Out of his heart will flow streams of living water

We can live for about 3 days without water but after that time elapses, chemical processes in the body begin to suffer and shut down from dehydration. The body is made up of approximately 60% water and is designed to constantly receive fresh water in order to sustain its life. In the same way the Holy Spirit within you is like a stream of fresh spiritual water flowing through your life.

Someone once said you can never put your foot in the same river twice because the water will always be different at any moment in time. As much as we would like to define and 'box off' God with our intellectual understanding, in reality He is an exciting, living, moving person who is beyond our limited human understanding.

Our experiences of God can vary greatly. Sometimes His presence feels like a powerful gushing white water river cascading down a mountain side, another time He may seem gentle like a river flowing through a wide valley. The Bible begins and ends with places where God dwells on earth and both of them are places from which rivers flow; the first is a garden[a] and the last is a wonderful shining city[b].

Ps 46:4 "There is a river whose streams make glad the city of God, the holy place where the Most High dwells."

Imagine the difference between a pond and a lake. The pond only fills up with water when it rains and then gradually dries up again. Ponds smell bad and accumulate decomposing waste; I wouldn't recommend taking a drink from one. On the other hand the lake receives water from rains and streams, but also has an outlet so that water can flow out again. Because of this the lake is full of sweet fresh water that keeps on flowing, but the pond is full of stagnant water that goes nowhere. Over and over again the Bible describes God as a stream of living (or moving) water. As we said in the first chapter, He is indeed present in your life, but you need to imagine His presence as a living lake rather than a stagnant pond.

a Gen 2, b Rev 22

Water

"Jesus said, 'If anyone is thirsty, let him come to me and drink. Whoever believes in me, as the Scripture has said, streams of living water will flow from within him.' By this he meant the Spirit, whom those who believed in him were later to receive." John 7:37-39

When you begin to let thanks flow to God from your heart you may imagine that it is part of this 'water of life' flow. Not only does God enjoy your praise and worship but it also does you a lot of good. When you worship God He receives thanks from you, but at the same time that very flow out of you enables God to pour into you. It imparts life to your soul. Good relationships are two way.

Something to do: *In your private times with God don't let your worship be only internal. Sometimes you can let your mouth audibly speak out His praise in thankfulness. This is letting the river flow out. Let your facial expressions reflect your emotions and let your body enhance your thanks with stances of kneeling or standing. Why not try raising your hands as an expression of surrender and receptivity? If you feel self conscious it's OK, nobody is looking except God! Let the spiritual stream of water flow and find expression in your physical body. The word 'rejoice' appears over one hundred times in the Bible; God wants us to be a people of joy!*

Worship is often a key part of any Christian activity because it aligns us with God's will and purpose and leads us into prayer. Prayer is not a stale, dry activity where we read God a list of our needs. It is like that stream of water we were talking about. Prayer is the very life of God flowing through your soul. When we come into line with God's heart through worship we arrive at a place where we can begin to hear His heart beat and sense His love and will. We can begin to pray for things that are important to Him and see things from God's perspective.

About Baptism in the Holy Spirit

Receiving the Holy Spirit is an important part of your life in Christ. You received Him when you asked Jesus to come into your life but it's important to keep being filled because He is vibrant and alive. Being filled with the Holy Spirit is sometimes called being baptised in the Holy Spirit because it's as if your whole being is immersed in His living waters. It can make you feel warm or disorientated, some people feel as if they need to lie down, others want to run around and shout for joy! Sometimes being filled with the Holy Spirit can happen quite spontaneously without anybody else around and at other times it can be because other Christians lay hands on you[a]. Ephesians 5:18 says, "Do

a Acts 9:17

not get drunk on wine, which leads to debauchery. Instead, be filled with the Spirit." The expression 'be filled' here is a present tense that means 'keep being filled'; baptism in the Spirit may start with an experience but it is meant to continue into your daily life.

God prayers

Imagine you are having a hard time because your neighbours are noisy and they wake you up with their arguing during the night. It makes you feel fearful. Initially you pray that God will make the noise stop and deliver you from being woken up at night. You ask Him to fix things by making them move away. However, after worshipping and giving thanks to God you begin to feel God's heart for these people. You begin to pray, "Lord, please help my neighbours..." As you feel your fear beginning to be replaced by faith, you continue, "Holy Spirit please come and fill their home with love and peace. Father God, restore their marriage and bring them a new love for each other." Can you see how one prayer is a pond that focuses on me and my needs and the other is a lake that flows out to touch others? The wonderful thing is that as you begin to pray 'God prayers' He doesn't just flow through you but begins to bring life and peace to your heart as well.

A heart open to the Lord will remain humble and teachable and allow God to mould it. Upon this foundation of trust we must let our faith in Jesus begin to find expression in the things we do, the decisions we make and the way we live our lives. Allow your faith to express itself and let the living waters flow.

Faith action

In his New Testament letter James points out that it makes no sense to say that you have faith in Jesus on the inside without it having an impact on what you do externally. He puts it so strongly that he states **"faith by itself, if it is not accompanied by action, is dead." James 2:17.** Your new relationship with God needs to find expression in what you say and do, otherwise your faith will be in danger of stagnating like a pool of water that has no flow.

Going back to our example of the noisy neighbours, it's very likely that if you begin to pray prayers that seek to bless your neighbours, God will give you a new attitude towards them as well. Formerly you were becoming bitter and resentful towards them but now you find yourself wondering if there's anything you can do to help them. When you see them struggling with a job in their garden you offer to help. This is streams of living water flowing from within you, or as James would say, real faith expressing itself through action.

Falling down

There will be times when you feel as though you have let the Lord down. You did something to save face before a critical friend or you swore and it instantly made you feel bad. What the Lord requires of you is not that you get everything right all the time but that you have a heart that is teachable and willing to learn. The Holy Spirit may prompt you to go back and say sorry to people; this may seem hard at first but it is very important that you respond.

Children must learn to walk but the parent doesn't scold them for falling down, neither does she leave the child on the floor. She helps her to get on her feet again. When you feel bad for letting God down, this is simply the Holy Spirit helping you up again. What counts in the Christian walk more than anything is not your ability to do everything perfectly but your resolve to get up and carry on if you know you got things wrong. You entered into the Christian life by recognising your need before God, never let that basic attitude slip away. It's so easy to begin to feel proud after a few small victories but never put yourself beyond God's discipline and correction.

"So then, just as you received Christ Jesus as Lord, continue to live in him, rooted and built up in him, strengthened in the faith as you were taught, and overflowing with thankfulness." Col 2:6-7

Being led by the Holy Spirit

There was once a guy who got saved who was, to all intents and purposes, a bit of a rogue. He ran a notorious bar where he regularly had strippers perform erotic dances for the customers. After a week his conscience began to bother him so he called up his local pastor to say he had decided to change his ways. As you can imagine the pastor was relieved to hear this, expecting that the Lord had convicted the new Christian about the dancers. "The thing is", the guy confessed to the pastor, "I think it's wrong to be watering down the beer, so from now on it's going to stop!"

The great thing about this story is that the guy is letting the Holy Spirit lead him at His own speed, one issue at a time. It's certain that if he continues to allow the Holy Spirit to guide him about his lifestyle that his subsequent choices will continue to honour God. Well-meaning Christians may be keen to tell you what you should and shouldn't be doing now you are saved, but true inner transformation can only come through the Holy Spirit.

Being led by the Holy Spirit is not the easy option. When you declared Jesus as your Lord and Saviour you effectively handed over the controls of your life to Him. In the past you lived your life by what you knew to be right and wrong, the law told you that. You knew it was wrong to steal another's bread because the law said so. But now you have been released from 'right and wrong' living into 'doing it out of love' living. This kind of living goes beyond simply keeping rules. **"We have been released from the law so that we serve in the new way of the Spirit." Romans 7:6**

Is it OK for Christians to...?

In life there are many choices that are not as clear cut as the law. Over and over again I have seen new Christians change their old empty habits, not because someone told them to, but simply because they don't feel right doing 'whatever it is' any more. They have had a change of view and now see what they used to do as hollow, empty activities. That may be happening to you because you are now sensitive to what pleases or displeases God. Can I encourage you to guard that new sensitivity as a matter of great priority? Don't ignore it or compromise it; if you do you will gradually stifle your relationship with God and may find that following Jesus becomes less of a loving relationship and more like a struggle to perform.

> ***Example scenario:*** *Jenny had been saved for just 2 weeks and instantly felt the Lord tell her to throw away the extreme horror films she used to collect and watch obsessively. No one told her to, she just felt the urge to have a clean sweep. She felt a great relief at having cleared them out of her life. However, one thing bothered her. She also had some movies that were 'not so bad', only 12A certificate and she sincerely wanted to know if it was OK for Christians to watch them. Here's the answer to this and many similar 'is this OK for Christians'? questions: Ask Jesus! You have an open line to heaven 24/7 and if you ask Him honestly you will have your answer.*

As human beings we would often much rather have a list of do's and don'ts. It seems a lot simpler but in reality this is external religion and has nothing to do with your new life in Christ. Ask Jesus if it's OK for you to engage in any number of activities (I am not suggesting you need to do this for activities which are obviously immoral or illegal[a]) and this is for sure... if your heart is truly to obey and honour Him, He will let you know! You will feel an inner peace or unease, depending upon His answer.

a Gal 5:19-23

Questions to think about:

1. Why is the presence of Jesus in your life more like a lake than a pond?

2. Have you taken the opportunity to express your faith yet? What did you do or say?

3. Have you any 'is it OK for Christians' questions? Have you asked Jesus what He thinks the answer is for you? What did you feel He said?

Chapter 3

food

Jesus said, "I am the bread of life"

Food is important for sustaining life. Not only does food provide energy for movement but also the building blocks for growth. After about three weeks without food your body will shut down as it begins to lack the nourishment it needs to function properly. Long before the three weeks is up your body will have begun to use energy in stored fats and other tissue in order to keep alive.

In the first two chapters I have emphasised the fact that you have a living relationship with God through His son Jesus Christ by virtue of the indwelling Holy Spirit. Because of His presence in you, you can know God through worship and prayer and faith action. However, there is yet another important way in which you can know God and that is through His written word, the Bible.

The words in the Bible were spoken into the hearts of certain people by God as special revelation. This revelation was then written down by those people as words with pen and ink to be passed on from generation to generation. We can now read the words in the Bible, and with the Holy Spirit's help, they can again become spiritual revelation to us about God. It is like digesting food. In order to benefit from the nutrients in the food we eat, we have to convert it into the substances our bodies need to live and grow. This process is called assimilation. In the same way, in order to benefit from the spirit and truth in the Bible we need to ask the Holy Spirit to make it spirit and truth to us as we read it.

Have you heard the expression, 'Babies do not come with an instruction manual'? Well the good news is that new Christian babies do. The Bible could be described as *'The Maker's instruction book for living'*. The God who created you has provided you with such a manual and it pretty well covers everything you need to know for living your life[a]. There is no doubt about it, the Bible is a very large book and a little intimidating for the new Christian. However, there are a lot of great resources available to help you get started.

a 2 Tim 3:16

About the Bible

The Bible is in fact a collection of books; 39 in the Old Testament and 27 in the New Testament. Some are history books, some are collections of poems, others are collections of wise sayings, and there are books of prophecy, letters and four gospels about the life of Jesus. It was written over a period of history starting from around fifteen hundred BC to the first century AD in different countries and languages. In its entirety the Bible wonderfully reveals to us the heart of God. It's divided into the Old Testament, written before Jesus was born, and the New Testament written after Jesus had ascended into heaven. Chapters and verse numbers were added to translations in the sixteenth century to help people more easily search and study the Scriptures. There is an old saying that the New Testament is in the Old Testament concealed, but the Old Testament is in the New Testament revealed. This means there is a thread of the gospel of Jesus that runs right through from the first book of Genesis all the way to Revelation. One of my previous church leaders was fond of saying that the Bible is like a stick of seaside candy: break it anywhere and it has the name of Jesus running through it![a]

a Thanks Geoff!

You are what you eat

It's important not only to eat often but also to have a good balanced diet. It's all too easy to read the Bible and make it say what we want to hear, or fit it to our own agenda. We can read the parts we like and leave the parts we don't like. This is akin to leaving your healthy greens and only eating desserts; it builds an unhealthy body. Try to be consistent with what you read. Yes, memorise the 'blessing' verses, but also read the chapter or even the whole book so that you know the context of the blessing. The main thing is to read it often and apply what you read to how you live your life. James 1:22-25 says that if you do that one thing you will be blessed in all that you do. It could be said that The Bible contains the seeds of life; if we come to it with faith and a teachable heart it becomes like daily bread to our soul.

> ***Something to do:** "All Scripture is God-breathed and is useful for teaching, rebuking, correcting and training in righteousness, so that the man of God may be thoroughly equipped for every good work." 2 Timothy 3:16-17*
>
> *Try memorising this verse. A good way to begin is to say each word on your fingers. For example, 'All Scripture is*

God-breathed' is five words that can be counted on one hand. Start with that. Take note of which word corresponds to which finger. Later on in the day try to remember the phrase again. You will find that using your fingers in this way helps you remember the five words. The same applies to the list of uses. There are five key words: teaching, rebuking, correcting, training and righteousness. You may find it useful to remember the first letters: TRCTR. Remember them with the fingers of one hand.

There is no easy way to remember the reference: 2 Timothy 3:16-17. Some people have a head for numbers (I'm not one of them). I'd be happy to know this verse was from 2 Timothy. However, in this case 3:16 is a well know chapter and verse for a quite a few popular Scriptures so that makes it a bit easier to remember.

Reading the Bible

You can find out what God is like and what His heart is for people by reading the Bible. If you don't have one yet, make it your priority to get one. It's the number one piece of physical kit for Christian survival. It may be expensive for your budget but worth every penny. The chances are that Christian friends will be only too glad to buy one for you, but if you have to make a sacrifice to get one it may be no bad thing, then it will hold even more value for you.

Suggested passages for a new Christian to read:

Try reading John's entire gospel. Then read Genesis chapters 1 to 3, Revelation chapters 20 to 22, Isaiah chapters 53 to 55, Matthew 5 to 7 (known as 'The Sermon on the Mount'), Romans chapters 5 to 8, all of Ephesians and all of James. Read the Psalms, many of which express the emotions and feelings we experience through the highs and lows of life. Read Proverbs for good, sound advice.

About Bibles

Bibles come in all printed shapes and sizes. Not only are there many different translations, there are also Bibles with study notes and reading guides. There are now 'themed' Bibles for just about anything you can think of, like 'Teens Bible' or 'Women's Bible' – published with certain covers or styles to suit a particular people group.

Most people have their favourite translation – it's usually the one they first got to know. The King James Version (KJV) is very old fashioned in its language (which is hardly surprising since it was written in the seventeenth century). On the other hand, 'The Message' by Eugene H. Peterson is a very modern easy to read translation (written in the 1990's), but not that good for serious study. Good modern translations include the New International Version (NIV), the New American Standard Bible (NASB) or the New King James Version (NKJV). Get one you will read and use and don't be afraid to mark it with notes and highlights and make it your own. Better to have a tatty, well used Bible full of marks and comments than one like new that never gets read.

There are also many web sites and apps that make digital Bibles available for your desktop or mobile phone. These are incredibly powerful and put a great host of translations and study resources at your fingertips. However, I believe there is something special about having a physical Bible book that you can get to know and make your own.

How often and how much of the Bible should I read?

The Bible is like spiritual food for the believer. Many Christians have Bibles, but very few read them regularly. Even if it is read regularly, it will not help you grow spiritually unless you ask the Holy Spirit to speak to you and you respond to what He says. Then you will build a strong foundation for your life in Jesus.

There are different ways to approach reading the Bible. Here are three:

1. Devotional Reading: For your daily bread

A devotional time is a certain period of time (usually in the morning before the working day starts) that you may set aside for Bible reading and prayer. You need to be realistic about how long this time should be. It can be anything from 5 minutes to 2 hours. I suggest 10 – 15 minutes is a good starting point. There are lots of daily devotional reading guides that will set out a Scripture reading, a couple of paragraphs that help you reflect on the passage and even a prayer guide. There are also audio resources so that you can listen to a portion of the Bible read every day.

The danger of devotional times is that they become ritualistic or worse still, like a lucky charm. This means that if you miss one you either feel guilty or fearful that you will have 'bad luck' all day. If you find this happening to you then please remember, it's not a sin to have no devotional time! It's not supposed to be a performance but a natural part of your relationship with Jesus. If you find that your planned devotional times are not working out for you don't beat yourself up about it. Your whole life is devoted to Jesus.

Combining reading the Bible with a time of worship and prayer is simply one way of allowing God to speak to you. Before you read ask Jesus to guide and teach you: **"Then he (Jesus)* opened their minds so they could understand the Scriptures." Luke 24:45,46**

2. Study Reading: To help your mind understand

The Bible is translated from different languages and cultures from over 2,000 years ago. It's therefore helpful to spend some time in study of Bible history, language and culture. To do this you may join a weekly study group at your church or download or buy study guide books (ask Christians you trust for advice on good ones – a sample list can be found at the back of this book). Understanding Scripture with your mind is called theology (literally 'study of God'). Some people enjoy this so much they go on to learn Greek and Hebrew and achieve academic qualifications in theology. This is not for everyone though and the danger is that it's possible to know the Scriptures inside out and yet have no living relationship with Jesus.

In John 5:39-40 Jesus said to the Scripture scholars of his day, "You diligently study the Scriptures because you think that by them you possess eternal life. These are the Scriptures that testify about me, yet you

* (Jesus) added

refuse to come to me to have life."

Scripture says that obedience to God is true wisdom[a], not simply the accumulation of knowledge. However, having a grasp of Bible times, customs and cultures is useful for understanding the Bible.

3. Bible Meditation: To help your 'heart' understand

Bible meditation is the opposite of Bible study. This is when you 'switch off your mind' and allow the Scripture to enter your 'heart' or inner being. Find a comfortable, quiet place to sit indoors or out, or maybe do this whilst walking. Take a portion of Scripture (for example Matthew 5:3-10, called the beatitudes or the blessings) and read the first verse:

"Blessed are the poor in spirit, for theirs is the kingdom of heaven."

Repeat the verse in your head until you have it memorised. Simply continue repeating the verse. Don't think about it or analyse it, just repeat it. This is called meditating on the Scripture. Your mind will want to wander away and think about other things but you must make it focus (meditate) on the verse; that is the discipline. After a while stop meditating on the verse and come to a place of quietness and just be attentive

a Prov 1:7

to the Lord. He may speak to you or He may not. It doesn't matter. What matters is that you are letting the Holy Spirit breathe life into your heart through the Scripture. This can be part of your devotional time.

Questions to think about:

1. Only reading favourite passages of the Bible and ignoring or rejecting the rest is like eating dessert and no greens. Why is this?

2. What is the difference between Bible study and Bible meditation?

3. Do you plan to have a time in your day for regularly reading and reflecting on Scripture? When and where do you think it will work for you to do that?

Chapter 4

shelter

You are a temple of the Holy Spirit

Humans have always lived in shelters of one sort or another – without shelter in some extreme climates human life is very vulnerable. As well as keeping the weather out, shelter also gives protection from enemies, wild animals and insects. Even if we have air, water and food we won't last long without protection from the elements. God provides us with protection, keeping us safe from things that may harm our life in Christ.

"But the Lord is faithful, and he will strengthen and protect you from the evil one." 2 Thessalonians 3:3

This doesn't mean that bad things never happen to Christians but it does mean **"that all things work**

**together for good to those who love God"
Romans 8:28**

Scripture says that your body is now the temple of the Holy Spirit[a]. Before Jesus asked the Father to send the Holy Spirit to the hearts of those who believed in Him, God's presence on earth had formerly manifested over a sacred box called the Ark of the Covenant[b]. If you have ever seen the movie 'Indiana Jones and The Raiders of the Lost Ark' you will know what I'm talking about[c]. This wooden box was completely encased in gold and had two figurines of cherubim (angels) stretching their wings out over it. The box was kept in the centre of the Jewish temple in an inner room called the Holy of Holies. It was such a sacred place that only the High Priest could enter; and even then only once a year[d]. The High Priest went in to speak with God on behalf of the people. There was a seemingly endless list of purification rituals and requirements he had to perform so that he could stand in the presence of the Holy God. There is even an ancient Jewish writing[e] that describes how a rope would be tied around his ankle so that if anything went wrong and he was burned up by God's Holy presence he could be dragged back out without endangering another's life!

a 1 Cor 6:19, b Ex 25:21, c Although the movie is fictional the ark is a real historical artefact, d Heb 9:7, e The Zohar 13th Century

Shelter

Now that same presence of God, that same awesome Holy Spirit, is dwelling in your body[a]. A little scary when you think about it isn't it!? And it is right to feel some holy fear of God. But the New Testament teaches us that we are now 'covered' or protected by the blood of the Lamb of God[b], His son Jesus Christ. It is through Him that we are counted righteous and holy and able to be a temple of the Holy Spirit. So therefore we can **"approach the throne of grace with confidence". Hebrews 4:16**

You may well ask, "Are we talking about God being my shelter or me being God's shelter here?" Well actually, it's both. The Holy Spirit is both inside of you and outside surrounding you as well. Imagine drawing a circle that represents your physical body. Initially you may picture that 'Christ in you' is like drawing another circle inside the one representing your body. A much more useful picture is to imagine that the outside circle is the Holy Spirit (He is not bound by time and space after all) and your body is the small circle within. He is both outside of you and inside you at the same time. That is how you can be the temple of the Holy Spirit and He can be your shelter and your strong tower as well[c]. He is God after all.

a Rom 8:11, b Rom 5:9, c Ps 61:3

The Gospel of freedom

One of the major divisions between Christianity and other major world faiths is not *if* we try to lead a good life but *why* we try to live a good life and make an effort to do the right thing. All other world faiths can broadly be said to have the belief that if you try hard to live a good life (honour God, be honest, give to the poor etc.) then God will reward you and you will hopefully get into heaven (no guarantees). Christians also believe that they should try to live a good life but their motivation is almost the opposite. They do good *because* God has already made them righteous and fit for heaven through the acceptable sacrifice of His son Jesus[a]. This is why we Christians do a lot of thanks and praise when we get together, particularly for the death and resurrection of Jesus! What an amazing gift God has given us in His son.

Because of this radical difference, one of the biggest accusations that Christianity had to answer when it first began was this: "If people can be declared righteous through faith alone then surely they can just go right on sinning without suffering the consequences (after all Jesus takes the rap for us doesn't He?)". In other words, the gospel of Jesus promotes immorality!

a Rom 5:19

The Apostle Paul takes great care to set the record straight in much of his New Testament letters, particularly the one to the Romans. He says that indeed Christians have been set free from trying to be righteous through their own efforts, but like a slave set free from a cruel master, our response is one of gratitude to God. Now we serve Him through love and devotion, knowing that He has already declared us righteous through Jesus Christ. We are free from fear about getting into heaven because Jesus' death and resurrection is our guarantee (instead of our performance)[a].

Lovers get more work done than workers

This means you are truly free. You are not tied to any external obligations such as special days or disciplines that treat the body harshly in order to be holy or righteous[b]. However, we have an obligation of love that goes beyond these external rules and regulations. Have you ever watched someone head over heels in love, doing a job for the object of their devotion? For example, let's say that the household rules require you to do the washing up, so you wash the dishes and you have fulfilled your duty. However, imagine that you are doing the washing up for someone you are crazy in love with. Let me tell you that not only are the dishes going to be cleaned, dried and put away, you would probably

a Romans chapters 5 to 8, b Col 2:16-23

clean the sink, the cupboards, mop the floor and perhaps finish it off with some fresh flowers on the window sill! That job is going to be done over and above what is required by the rules. The fact is that 'lovers get more work done than workers'. The Bible says **"Whatever you do, work at it with all your heart, as working for the Lord, not for men" Col 3:23** – this is how we use our freedom in Christ.

The Bible is clear that Christians should have nothing to do with acts of the sinful nature:

"The acts of the sinful nature are obvious: sexual immorality, impurity and debauchery; idolatry and witchcraft; hatred, discord, jealousy, fits of rage, selfish ambition, dissensions, factions and envy; drunkenness, orgies, and the like." Galatians 5:19-21

This may come as a shock to you but nothing can remove the blessing and protection of God on your life now you are a Christian except one thing: you! Your own wilful disobedience to the Holy Spirit is the only thing on earth that can remove the blessing of God. Let me be clear about this; I did not say that you could remove God's love from your life. Nothing can separate you from the love of God[a]. What I am talking about here are His benefits and blessings. Again, it is not that

a Rom 8:38-39

God requires or expects you to get everything right but that your heart is for Him and not against Him. The reason I put your relationship with God as your priority in the first two chapters of this booklet is that this should be the motivation for your obedience, not some list of things that you can and can't do. These 'acts of the sinful nature' remove God's protection over your life because it is tantamount to going back to your old cruel master (sin and death) and telling him to beat you up some more! God allows you to have that free will because He will not force you to serve and love Him.

About Communion

Because our righteousness comes from Jesus, we can begin to understand how important the Communion bread and wine are to the believer. When we take these by faith we are saying that we embrace the mystery of being united with Christ in His death and resurrection. Communion is also an act of obedience to Jesus' command to 'do this in remembrance of me'[a], an outward sign of your identification with His death and resurrection. The bread symbolises His body and the wine symbolises His blood. Talk to your mentor or church leader about taking the communion and be sure to take part as an act of your new Christian faith.

a Luke 22:19

How to use your freedom

The apostle Paul wrote to new Christians explaining that they now had great freedom, but this freedom was to be led by the Holy Spirit and produce His good fruit:

"But the fruit of the Spirit is love, joy, peace, patience, kindness, goodness, faithfulness, gentleness and self-control. Against such things there is no law."
Galatians 5:22-24

Being the temple of the Holy Spirit means that we are valued by a loving heavenly Father (**"I will be a Father to you, and you will be my sons and daughters, says the Lord Almighty" 2 Cor 6:18**). This truth brings us out of any condemnation or thought of not being good enough and into a place of acceptance and security. Now we neither have to promote ourselves or put ourselves down. Now we can love people from a place of security instead of a place of insecurity. This means that we don't need to fear rejection from others because our sense of value no longer needs to come from other people. We can love and value others because we know that God loves and values us.

Read Matthew 18 verses 21 to 35. In this passage Jesus uses a parable to explain to Peter that there should be no limit on a Christian's mercy because they have been shown the ultimate mercy by God. It is important not to judge others as if your goodness came from your own efforts; this is called self righteousness.

Because we know we are loved by God we can honour the different opinions of others without feeling threatened. We can be the first to say sorry when we have upset someone. We can forgive others for hurting us. We can be careful to respect and look after other people's property. We can be hard working and trusted employees even for a difficult boss.

Circumstances don't define you, they simply reveal who you are. Jesus said that it's not what goes into a man's mouth that makes him unclean but what comes out of his mouth when he speaks[a]. The way you behave in difficult circumstances will show you what areas of your life you need to submit to the Holy Spirit. Use words that honour the presence of the Holy Spirit in your life. Don't criticise and put people down; don't gossip about them behind their backs but honour people as if they were better than you. This pleases the Holy Spirit and allows Him to promote you because you are not promoting yourself[b].

a Matt 15:11, b James 4:10

When being a Christian seems hard

If you find yourself from time to time thinking that being a Christian is hard you are not alone. There is a great metaphor in the Bible for the transition you have made from unbeliever to believer. The book of Exodus tells the story of how the people of Israel were led by Moses out of slavery in Egypt into the wilderness. They had come out from the terrible oppression of slavery by many great miracles from God (see Exodus 14). However, even though they had seen the miracles and initially trusted Moses they soon began to grumble and miss their life of toil. The people of Israel had evidently come out of Egypt but it was proving even harder to get Egypt out of the people of Israel. They began to say, "Why is being God's special people so hard?" Sometimes this is how new Christians can begin to feel.

God is like a good parent who removes things from a small child because he is not yet ready to handle them. The child doesn't always understand why he can't play with the matches. The story in Exodus reminds us that God needed to teach the people how to trust and rely on Him for everything so that they would be ready for their wonderful land of inheritance, 'a land of milk and honey'. He had to begin teaching them in the wilderness how to stop thinking like slaves and start thinking like His special chosen people, His royal family.

Shelter

Imagine your life is a house. When you came to God it was in pretty bad shape. We can often make the mistake of thinking that God wants to come into the house of our lives and do a lovely renovation job; fix up the roof, put in a new kitchen and a new bathroom suite. However, the Bible teaches us that God's redemptive plan is not so much to do a restoration job on our lives as to knock it down, to clear away the rubble and start again! That is what has happened to you – you are a new creation. Your old sinful nature has gone, it is dead and it has been crucified with Christ[a].

If you find yourself thinking that it's hard to be a Christian, the chances are that you are struggling to really trust that Jesus has made you completely righteous and acceptable to God. It is only from this one simple gospel truth that we can be released from earning our salvation and be set free from our old sinful nature. Paul says in Romans 12, "Do not conform any longer to the pattern of this world, but be transformed by the renewing of your mind." If you think you are 'a sinner trying to be good' then you will struggle like 'a sinner trying to be good'. However the truth is that Scripture says you are now the righteousness of Christ set free by the cross to enjoy a wonderful God loving life[b].

a Rom 6:6-7, b Rom 6:20-23

About Baptism

Believer's Baptism in water is a Christian act that symbolises personal repentance (a turning away from sin) and belief in Jesus as saviour. I call it 'Believer's Baptism' because, unlike the christening of a baby, it requires that the individual understands the gospel message and confesses and acts upon it for themselves. Immersion in water is a symbol of dying with Christ, and emergence from the water a symbol of being raised with Him to eternal life[a]. Just as the people of Israel passed through the Red Sea, baptism is a way of saying 'I have left my life of slavery behind and now I am free in Jesus'. If you have not been baptised as a believer please speak to a trusted Christian mentor and seriously consider it — it will strengthen your Christian life. Baptism is an outward expression of what has happened to you on the inside and a public identification with Jesus.

---

a Col 2:11 & 12

Questions to think about:

1. What is the main difference between a Christian trying to do good and those of other beliefs trying to do the same?

2. Why do lovers get more work done than workers?

3. What is the only thing that can remove God's protection and blessing from your life?

4. Do you have areas in your life that you are finding hard to leave behind? Ask God to show you how completely He has dealt with your old life through the cross of Jesus. Begin to trust God that your old sinful self is dead and has no power over you any more. Ask the Lord to show you how much He loves you and what a great plan He has for your life.

Chapter 5

purpose

God... put him in the Garden of Eden to work it and take care of it

We have covered the most basic needs for our survival: air, water, food and shelter and seen how these apply to our 'life in Christ'. Yet there are other elements the human soul needs in order to thrive and prosper and one of these is having a purpose. Without fruitful, purposeful work, people lack vision and motivation to achieve. They become prone to depression, isolation and sickness. Work elevates the human being from simply existing, to having a life of achievement and significance. We were created and commanded by God to care for the world and be fruitful[a] and that mandate has not changed. We are created for purpose, to apply our energy to nurturing life and be good stewards of what our heavenly Father has given us.

a Genesis chapters 1 & 2

It's a mistake to think that once you are saved, your lot in life is to keep on the straight and narrow, go to church, put money in the Sunday collection and ride the 'salvation train' out of here to paradise. That is an escapist attitude which departs from the teaching of the Bible that says heaven and the reign of King Jesus are actually coming to earth. The business of the Christian is the business of the Lord Jesus. He taught us to pray to our heavenly Father, "Your will be done on earth as it is in heaven[a]." God is not just working in your life to help you alone, but to help others through you, to transform and affect the world you live in. There is more to being a Christian than just waiting for your ticket to heaven.

One of the number one questions people ask themselves has to be, 'Why am I here?' or 'What is the point of my existence?' If you are still breathing and alive on planet Earth then God certainly has a reason for you to be here. The Bible says **"for it is God who works in you to will and to act according to his good purpose." Phil 2:13.** He has a good plan and a purpose for your life[b].

God has made you unique, there is only one of you, you are the best you there is! Only you have your unique mix of personality and experience, living in your particular time and place. He has given you abilities

a Matt 6:10, b Jer 29:11

that you did not earn or deserve; they are a gift from God. From having great people skills to a talent for mathematics, they can all be used to honour and glorify Him.

Works of service

The Bible says that Jesus gave leaders to His people to equip believers for 'works of service'[a]. Did you catch that? It means that all Christians are called to do ministry. Don't make the mistake of thinking that unless you are working for a church or in a church building that your work is not spiritual. You have Jesus living inside you now and all your life is rooted in the spiritual. Yes there should be special times in your schedule for fellowship and devotional activities to God but that doesn't mean God does not want to be involved in the rest of your week. The Bible says that **"the earth is the Lord's and everything in it" Ps 24:1**; it all belongs to Him! If you are a musician he wants to be involved with your music, if you are a teacher he wants to be involved with you in the classroom, if you are a mechanic, if you are a home-maker, student, scientist, employment seeker, accountant, volunteer, manager... you get the picture?

So what does serving the Lord mean in everyday life? It

a Eph 4:11 & 12

means that the most menial task can have meaning and significance. Even when no one else knows what you are doing you can serve God to the best of your ability no matter what, in the knowledge that He is a good God who sees and rewards devotion and diligence.

Doing your best

> ***Read Matthew chapter 25 verses 14-30*** *- 'The Parable of the Talents'.*

In this parable Jesus shows how each one of us is given gifts or talents by God to be used to the best of our ability, He doesn't expect any more or any less. He is the powerful, awesome God of the universe but the story shows that His heart is to prosper us and not to harm us. It is as if He searches the earth looking for people He can reward. Those servants who have done their best are given a threefold blessing. First they are given praise by their master, "Well done good and faithful servant!" What better motivation can we have to work hard than the personal gratitude of our God? Then each servant who has tried hard is promoted and given more responsibility, "You have been faithful with a few things, I will put you in charge of many things." What could give you a greater sense of significance than having God Himself increase your influence and authority? And finally, as if that wasn't enough, they are each invited to share in God's joy, "Come and share your master's happiness!" Now that is a party worth going to.

The servant who did not do well was guilty of one thing - being lazy. He did not make any effort at all with the gifts he was given. He was also cowardly. He did not want to take any risks or make himself vulnerable by trying to improve his prospects. It is tempting for Christians to hide behind a pretence of false humility in the name of preferring others. Phrases like, "I'm not good enough", or "nobody wants to hear what I've got to say", come easily... yet the reality is we often find excuses for staying in our comfort zones and not stepping out.

The servants in the story are all servants of God so this parable is not about getting into heaven. That is certainly not to do with our own efforts (as we discovered in chapter one). This parable is about heavenly rewards for what we do with the time and resources given to us. The servant who was lazy becomes full of deep regret and bitterness. I don't know about you but when I stand before my Lord in the future I'd love to hear the words, "Well done good and faithful servant!"

Gifts and talents

There are many different gifts spoken of in the New Testament. Some are to do with natural gifting such as the gift of helps or administration. Then there are those that are more spiritual sounding, like the gift of special faith or the gifts of healing. The main thing to remember about any gift you may have is that it is a *gift*. You did not earn it or deserve it in any way and it does not make you more important than anyone else.

This is the message in 1 Corinthians chapter 12 when the Apostle Paul wrote to a young community of Christians who were falling out with each other over who was the most important. Was it those who could discern what was going on spiritually or was it those who could do miracles? What do you think? Paul said it was neither. He said to ask that question was rather like saying, "What is more important, the eye or the ear?" The answer is that the body needs both. The Holy Spirit gives different gifts to different people so that they need to rely on each other and be more effective together.

The other thing to remember about your spiritual gifts is that they are not primarily meant for you. The reason the Holy Spirit may give you a gift of healing is that there is someone else who needs to be made well, or the Holy Spirit may give you a gift of wisdom because another person has a difficult problem to solve. The gifts are spiritual empowerments to help you reach out to a hurting, lost world with the love and power of Jesus. You are to be a living expression of the reality of God's love and power to those who do not know Him like you now do.

"And God is able to make all grace abound to you, so that in all things at all times, having all that you need, you will abound in every good work." 2 Cor 9:8

Something to do: *Have a look through the following list. How many of these words do you think describe you? (Don't worry if you don't know the exact meaning of every word)...*

Administrative, pioneering, creative, spiritually discerning, encouraging, evangelistic, exhorter, full of faith, generous, healer, helper, hospitable, intercessor, prophetic, leader, compassionate, miracle worker, missionary, musical, pastoral, disciplined, teacher, speaker of spiritual languages, wise, writer...?

Now read through the list again more slowly and this time ask God what He thinks best describes you; it may be different.

Being fruitful

Spiritual fruit in your character looks like the 'fruit of the Spirit' in Galatians 5:22-23 (love, joy, peace, patience, kindness, goodness, faithfulness, gentleness and self-control), but there are other types of spiritual fruit. Seeing others come to salvation and be born again is one type. Then there are those characteristics of the Kingdom of God that seemed to accompany Jesus wherever He went; all kinds of healings and deliverance, restoration of the downcast and hope for the poor. How about the provision of clean drinking water or educational resources in a community? What about a women's refuge or a medical centre? Did you know that the majority of our health and education services in the west were originally established through church ministries? Francis of Assisi said, "Preach the gospel at all times and if necessary use words." Wherever the gospel is demonstrated, suffering should be relieved and people blessed, as this is also spiritual fruit.

Work is always more rewarding when we know to what purpose we are working. Listen to this story: There were three stone masons working on a cathedral and each was asked by a passer-by what he was doing. The first stone mason replied, "I'm carving a stone." The second glanced over at the emerging structure and said, "I'm building a cathedral." While the third stone mason lifted his eyes to heaven and said, "I'm glorifying God!" All three were performing the same basic task but they had three very different perspectives.

When it comes to our work, whatever that may be, as believers we can know that we are serving God and therefore, just like the third stone mason, doing whatever we are doing for His glory. So whether you are cleaning toilets or performing brain surgery **'whatever you do, do it all for the glory of God.' 1 Corinthians 10:31-32**. If His approval and pleasure is your goal, you will do your best, and if you feel as though your boss is a slave driver then this Scripture is for you:

'Slaves, obey your earthly masters in everything; and do it, not only when their eye is on you and to win their favour, but with sincerity of heart and reverence for the Lord. Whatever you do, work at it with all your heart, as working for the Lord, not for men, since you know that you will receive an inheritance from the Lord as a reward. It is the Lord Christ you are serving.' Col 3:22-25

It's important to know your purpose and destiny, where you are going and how you are going to get there. For the Christian, our ultimate *destiny* is to become like Jesus and to share in His glory[a]. On the other hand our *purpose* is how we are going to get there and the nature and place of how we are to serve on the way. While we focus on the challenges and achievements of our purpose, God shapes us into the character of our destiny, into the likeness of Christ.

Purpose and destiny

I am no expert on gardening but I have been told that a banana tree will not grow bananas if it is planted outdoors here in the UK. The same is true of some of our indigenous species of plants, they would not thrive and be fruitful in tropical places. In a similar way God has a purpose for your life that will provide the perfect circumstances in which you can be fruitful.

Are you where God wants you to be? Is there a call on your life to serve in a certain profession or a specific place? Pray about these things. Don't let life pass you by without ever finding what God has called you to do. The fact is that we all serve somebody and will all serve some purpose. The purpose God has for you may not necessarily be anything profound or glamorous but if God has called you to it, it will be rewarding, even if it is hard work. Prosperity has very little to do with how

a Eph 4:13 & 2 Thes 2:14

Purpose

much you have, but it has everything to do with who you are. Don't be a preacher if He called you to be a plumber, don't be a city banker if He called you to live and serve in a remote rural community. Be what God has put in your heart and called you to be.

Questions to think about

1. What gifts and resources has God given you to use and look after?

2. Are you able to serve Jesus in your daily chores, activities or employment? Do you think you are where God wants you to be?

3. Do you have a dream or an ambition you feel God has give you? What is it?

Chapter 6

community

Let us not give up meeting together

Now we have everything for a healthy Christian life except one last vital ingredient; other people to share it with. People are created to be communal, to live in families and tribes and to be social creatures. It's clear from Scripture that what God had in mind from the beginning was a family to call His own[a]. Without healthy, meaningful relationships people can often become isolated and depressed. However we were created to be part of community.

Significant relationships

Before we talk about church let's have a quick look at those relationships you are in already: parents, siblings, children, girlfriend, boyfriend, best friend or

a Gen 1:28

partner. These are people who share and have a significant influence in your life at one level or another. It's important that you tell these people that you have become a Christian and have decided to live your life in a new way. If you already know Christians among these relationships then obviously you would expect some encouragement and enthusiasm from them. However, if you are alone in coming to Christ among your peers then you may have to prepare your heart for less encouraging responses, like this one, "Oh, so you've got religion now? I'll give that a week!"

Your closest friends and family may become your worst critics, but the truth is they are watching you to see if what you've got is the 'real deal'. On the one hand they may be teasing you with questions like, "I didn't know you were allowed to do that now you're a Christian?" and the next moment when you display some new moral integrity, "... holier than thou are you? We're not good enough for you any more, huh?" It's unpleasant but don't be intimidated. Working out your faith in the context of these relationships may be one of your biggest challenges, but also, if you let God use them, one of the most effective ways God will work in your heart and impact those around you.

a Mat 6:10, b Jer 29:11

The fact is that those closest to us feel threatened when their influence over us is diminished. When you acknowledged Jesus as your Saviour and said 'yes' to God you also effectively said 'no' to all the other 'gods' that you had allowed to have precedence over your life. These 'gods' range from the more obvious such as obsessive hobbies, to the less obvious, for example, people who you have allowed to influence and control you. It often boils down to this, (and you may actually be challenged with this question), "OK, so who is more important to you, me or God?" What you must settle in your heart is that the Lord God has first place in your heart, above everything else. The danger is that if you allow another to be more important than God in any area, you are effectively making that person your god and that is a recipe for disaster in any relationship.

Control

We live in an age of control. We become accustomed to picking up the TV remote, pressing the button and getting what we want instantly. But when it comes to relationships, where there is control there will always be an element of punishment or fear; "If you don't do what I want I will make your life miserable". But Scripture says that you have been set free from the 'fear factor':

1 John 4:18 "There is no fear in love. But perfect love drives out fear, because fear has to do with punishment. The one who fears is not made perfect in love."

As a Christian you have been called to follow the way of love[a], which means not only do you no longer have to control others, but you yourself no longer have to be controlled by fear. You may choose to do something another person wants you to, but the key thing is to choose it out of love. In the case of your relationship with the Holy Spirit you are allowing Him to guide you because you know that He gives you that choice; He operates out of perfect love. God did not force you to love Him. He loved you first[b] and then invited you to love Him back. He modelled the way of love for you so you can bring that same love into your relationship with others[c].

The challenge for those with an unsaved spouse is always to try and walk the path between spiritual integrity and sacrificial love. They must learn how to honour their partner without compromising their faith in God, trying to avoid being self-righteous and judgemental. The unsaved spouse will be watching to see if this 'religion stuff' works and providing the other with many opportunities to grow in grace. Christians with unsaved partners always long for

a 1 Cor 14:1, b John 3:16, c Mat 5:43-45

Community

them to come to know the Lord but this must not be achieved through control... keep praying and let the Holy Spirit do His work.

Whenever I hear a young Christian say that they have a new girlfriend or boyfriend who is not a believer but is 'cool about me being a Christian', I have often watched as their faith has gradually been eroded away. If you are single and have a choice about who you are going to spend the rest of your life with, please take seriously the Bible's advice that to be joined so profoundly with someone who cannot share your life in Christ will make your faith walk so much harder[a]. This is not to say that a married couple who are both Christians will not have all the challenges that come to any marriage, but they can face them with prayer and assurance that God is in control and in all things works for the good of those who love Him[b].

The worldwide Church

Sadly a big reason why many people reject Jesus is that they can't stand the church. Even if you do come to the Lord you may feel that other Christians are such an odd collection of people that you really don't want to be associated with them. However, despite the fact that you may be tempted to think you don't need

a 2 Cor 6:14, b Rom 8:28

other Christians, you really do. Having an 'it's just me and God' attitude is not as spiritual as it sounds. You need other Christians around you and they need you, it's the primary way in which God will help you grow up in your faith.

The Bible describes the church as the body of Christ with Jesus as the head[a]. Because the church is made up of people who have Christ in them, in a sense the church collectively represents the embodiment of Jesus on the earth. For all its flaws (and there are many), to love Jesus is to love His body the church.

The church is made up of people of all sorts of character and personalities, all ages, and all kinds of backgrounds and the Bible describes us as living stones. We are not like mass manufactured bricks coming out of a factory like clones. We are all unique individuals who need each other. If you build a wall with different shaped stones there are only certain stones that will fit in certain places. No one else can fill your spot! The very reason the church needs you is that you are different from them, not because you are the same! Churches where everyone has to be the same, dress the same and talk the same are missing the point. God delights in diversity – just look at the variety in creation.

a Col 1:18

Community

Can I choose the wrong church?

The church is the worldwide community of all believers in Jesus. It's popular today to express a belief that all ways lead to God and mix up what the Bible says with other religious writings and philosophies, but this is a dangerous view. How can we say with surety that if someone professes Mickey Mouse to be God that they are wrong? We have to draw the line somewhere between truth and error. One of the main ways to do this is to use the Bible as a 'plumb line' of truth; but even here there are so many different interpretations and translations it's easy to get misled. One sure way is to have a statement of Christian core beliefs that is based on the essentials of true Christianity. One of the oldest and most universally accepted statements of the orthodox Christian faith is the Nicene Creed[a] which includes the virgin birth, the trinity of God, the death and resurrection of Jesus Christ and the return of Jesus to judge all people. Try to make sure that the church you join holds to this basic statement of faith.

About 'Christian' Sects

'Christian' sects depart from the orthodox Christian church by holding to core doctrinal beliefs that are not

[a] See 'further reading'

> in the Nicene Creed. Two of the biggest 'Christian' sects are Mormons (Church of the Latter Day Saints) and Jehovah's Witnesses (Watch Tower Publications). Amongst other errors these sects do not believe that Jesus is God incarnate but a lesser being.

The local church

Despite the fact that the church is a massive multi-cultural, multi-linguistic spiritual family, it's good for you to be part of a local community of believers where you live. It's not enough to simply chat to other Christians on an internet social network site (even if you have over 1,000 friends ;-).

Hebrews 10:24-25 says "And let us consider how we may spur one another on toward love and good deeds. Let us not give up meeting together, as some are in the habit of doing, but let us encourage one another — and all the more as you see the Day approaching."

The church is not the building. Unfortunately even those of us who know this still betray the belief by saying, "Let's go to church," or, "I'll see you at church" on a regular basis. It's just so much part of our tradition. However, the church building is not the church, the church is the people. In fact a church can meet in a building without a steeple and still be a church. It can just be a community of people who meet in each other's homes and still be the church. How do I know this? Because this is exactly how the church began in the first century[a], just by meeting in each other's homes. A local church then is simply a community of believers who love and support one another.

About denominations and styles of local church

There are many different denominations and expressions of church. For example, there is the Catholic Church, the Church of England (Anglican), the Baptist church, Evangelical churches, Methodist and Pentecostal, to name just a few. To make matters more confusing there are churches that are 'non-denominational' or 'independent', which are often linked with other churches in mutual support networks (like the Evangelical Alliance). Denominations tend to have their own emphasis in their beliefs. For example, Baptists are known for their adherence to adult water baptism and Evangelicals for their emphasis on Bible teaching.

As well as this you may come across many different styles of worship in different churches. For example, an Anglican church may be very formal with hymns and

a Acts 2:46

liturgies that are spoken by the vicar who dresses in robes. These prayers and statements of belief are then repeated solemnly by the congregation. At the other end of the spectrum you can find an Anglican Church that is very informal and expressive in style; the vicar wears jeans and there are drums, guitars, hand clapping and hands raised in worship (something you might hear called 'happy-clappy!')

There is great variety within the Christian faith – none of them is right or wrong, they are simply different expressions of worship, teaching and fellowship.

I have made the 'questions to think about' at the end of this chapter things to consider when joining a local church. Whether it is in the home or under a steeple, I hope you will find the church family where you can truly belong and grow strong in your faith.

Community

Questions to think about

Here are some helpful points to consider when looking for a church:

1. **Where does the Lord want me to be part of a Christian community of believers?**
   You may think it is your choice to pick and choose a church to go to but it isn't, it is the Lord's. He has exactly the right church family for you to be part of – it may not be the place you would choose but you need to know that this is where the Holy Spirit says, "Yes!" Why don't you pray and make sure you have God's peace about it. Otherwise you may fall into the deadly trap of 'church hopping', just going from one church to another and never truly belonging anywhere.

2. **Where does the person who led me to Jesus go to church? Where do they think I should go?**
   Most people are introduced to Jesus through a friend who has prayed and cared for them over a period of time. If this is true for you then your friend will also care about your spiritual safety and growth. Their opinion counts too, especially if they continue to help you in your faith walk.

3. **Is this community part of the physical community where I live?**

   Churches can come in many shapes and forms. Some people will travel a long way to meet with a church family God has joined them to. However, I encourage you to try to be part of a church where you live so that it will be easier to share life with your brothers and sisters in Christ outside of meetings. I often meet my church family when I am buying provisions at my local shop. It makes a big difference to my day. If you know that God is calling you to a church across town why not pray about moving to live closer?

4. **Do I think I will grow strong in my faith at this church?**

   You need to be in a church which will not only encourage you in your faith but will also stretch and challenge you too. The worship style may not be your particular taste but does it draw you into God's presence? The preaching and teaching may not be the most eloquent but do you find yourself encouraged and challenged? The people may not be 'your type' but do they help you to cultivate love and faith in God? The leaders may not be perfect but do you feel you can respect and trust them?

Community

5 . Is it a place where I can help and serve others?
You are not primarily part of a local church to get something. Don't make the mistake of thinking that because you turn up and give money that you are a stakeholder who should have a say in how things are run and what you should get out of it. You are there to serve others and be a blessing and encouragement to the church family. Join a church where there are plenty of opportunities to give financially and serve others.

And so you will begin to appreciate that the church is a community of believers who can express the love of Jesus to you, as well as you to them, and in this way we have come full circle. We began our booklet with the most vital element for Christian survival - 'Christ in you, the hope of glory'. Now we end with what it means to love and appreciate Jesus in others.

Being a Christian is essentially the art of learning how to love. Learning how to love God, learning how to love others and so learning how to love yourself as God meant you to be.

afterword

I hope this booklet has been an encouragement to you. I imagine, like an adventurer, your hands are stacked full of everything you will need for your survival pack: air, water, food, shelter, a mission and a support team. Setting out on a new journey is often a mixture of concerns and emotions but in the Holy Spirit we have more than a map, we have the living God journeying with us to guide and equip us.

So what more can I give you to help you on your exciting adventure of life in Christ? Only to repeat this pearl of wisdom again:

"Trust in the Lord with all your heart, and lean not on your own understanding; in all your ways acknowledge Him, and He shall direct your paths." Proverbs 3:5-6 NKJV

I would like to finish this booklet by praying for you:

"Father I thank you for this dear reader; my brother or sister in the Lord Jesus. I rejoice that they have chosen

to follow you and make it their life's goal to know you more and more. Thank you for beginning a good work in them and that you will complete what you have started. Thank you for providing everything they need to be established and grow strong in their faith and that you are with them and have promised to never leave or forsake them. Help them with the challenges that come. Help them understand that they begin from a place of victory and to trust in you in everything. I pray that they will not be robbed of the blessings of heaven but would have the strength to make the best choices, motivated out of love rather than obligation. Give them the courage to honour you in all they say and do. Teach them Holy Spirit how to hear and act upon your guidance. Unite them with brothers and sisters in Jesus who will want their best and help them to thrive and grow in the gifts you have given them. Most of all Lord, help them to trust in you with all their heart and lean not on their own understanding and to acknowledge you in all their ways. Bless them Lord Jesus. Amen."

Please feel free to visit **www.SpiritLifestyle.com** and let me know how you are doing…

recommended further reading

Chapter 1: Air

On the atonement: **The Cross of Christ** by John Stott (Inter-Varsity Press)

On the Christian walk: **Pilgrims Progress** by John Bunyan (Moody Publishers)

On grace: **What's so Amazing about Grace?** by Philip Yancey (Zondervan)

On God's characteristics: **Knowing God** by J.I. Packer (Hodder and Stoughton)

Chapter 2: Water

On living faith: **The Practice of the Presence of God** by Brother Lawrence (Merchant Books)

On prayer: **Experiencing the Depths of Jesus Christ** by Jeanne Guyon (Christian Books)

On Christian disciplines: **The Celebration of Discipline** by Richard Foster (Hodder & Stoughton)

Chapter 3: Food

On Understanding the Bible: **Unlocking the Bible** by David Pawson (Collins)

On how to study the Bible: **Rick Warren's Bible Study Methods** by Rick Warren (Zondervan)

Daily Devotionals:

Word for Today is a free quarterly daily devotional resource from United Christian Broadcasters (UCB). It is also available as a daily email subscription from www.ucb.co.uk

Essential 100 Group Study Guide by Scripture Union. Read through the Bible in 100 readings. Visit: www.scriptureunion.org.uk

Read the Bible in a Year: **The One year Bible NIV** (Tyndale House Publishers)

YouVersion: **Bible App** www.youversion.com

Chapter 4: Shelter

On spiritual protection: **Enemy Access Denied** by John Bevere (Charisma House)

On Christ centred living: **There were Two Trees in the Garden** by Rick Joyner (MorningStar Publications)

On living free: **Steps to Freedom in Christ** by Neil T Anderson (Monarch Books)

Chapter 5: Purpose

On the gifts of the Spirit: **Gifts of the Spirit** by Derek Prince (Whitaker House)

On finding your purpose: **The Purpose Driven Life** by Rick Warren (Zondervan)

On supernatural living: **The Normal Supernatural Christian Life** by Aliss Cresswell (55:11)

Chapter 6: Community

On family relationships: **Loving On Purpose** by Danny Silk (Destiny Image)

On expressions of church: **Streams of Living Water** by Richard Foster (Eagle Publishing)

The Nicene Creed

I believe in one God, the Father Almighty, Maker of heaven and earth, and of all things visible and invisible.

And in one Lord Jesus Christ, the only-begotten Son of God, begotten of the Father before all worlds; God of God, Light of Light, very God of very God; begotten, not made, being of one substance with the Father, by whom all things were made.

Who, for us men and for our salvation, came down from heaven, and was incarnate by the Holy Spirit of the virgin Mary, and was made man; and was crucified also for us under Pontius Pilate; He suffered and was buried; and the third day He rose again, according to the Scriptures; and ascended into heaven, and sits on the right hand of the Father; and He shall come again, with glory, to judge the quick and the dead; whose kingdom shall have no end.

And I believe in the Holy Ghost, the Lord and Giver of Life; who proceeds from the Father and the Son; who with the Father and the Son together is worshipped and glorified; who spoke by the prophets.

And I believe in one holy catholic and apostolic Church. I acknowledge one baptism for the remission of sins; and I look for the resurrection of the dead, and the life of the world to come. Amen

1662 Version from the Anglican Book of Common Prayer

thanks

My gratitude and thanks to all who helped me put this booklet together. Aliss you are such an inspiration and encouragement, Hazel for sorting out my semicolons from my commas, mum and dad for wise advice and being the role models that you are and Danny for clarifying subtle theological nuances.

A special mention goes out to David Dean. You were my 'Believer's Guide to Survival' when I got saved; thanks for investing in me.

about the author

Rob Cresswell along with his wife Aliss pioneer ministries which seek to engage people where they are and demonstrate the love and power of God.

Rob received Jesus as his personal saviour in 1976 at the age of ten during a 'Come Together' gospel concert in Derbyshire UK.

After graduating from ministry school in 2006 they established a local church in their home town of Chester and several exciting outreach initiatives (known for salvations, healings and miracles) including a café, shop and B&B.

In 2014 they founded **Spirit Lifestyle**, a training and equipping organisation focussing on the gifts of the Spirit utilising online multimedia resources for peer to peer evangelism and discipleship training.

Rob & Aliss continue to write, present, train and travel, spreading the gospel and pioneering Kingdom initiatives internationally.

Don't just Survive: Thrive!

The Believer's Guide to THRIVING

Fruit that will last — ANCIENT PATHWAYS to personal freedom — FOR DEEPER ROOTS

Rob Cresswell

Watch Rob present

The **Believer's Guide** to **SURVIVAL**
— *Video Series* —

on
SpiritLifestyle.com

More Books from Rob & Aliss Cresswell

Training in Supernatural Living

with Rob & Aliss Cresswell

- ▶ **Video Library:** instant access to quality training
- 👥 **Members Community:** for friendship and support
- 🔊 **Monthly Livestream Q&A:** with Rob & Aliss
- 🎬 **Weekly Classes:** coaching for spirit, soul and body
- ☺ **Name Your Amount:** subscription & free trial
- 🎟 **PLUS!** Local classes and cafés

We'd love to see you! *Rob + Aliss.*

SpiritLifestyle.com

miracle.cafe
a taste of heaven

For all the latest news and stories from our Miracle Cafés

www.miracle.cafe

@miraclecafes